AF409344

Basics on Public Key Infrastructure (PKI)

By A. Scholtens

Writer: A. Scholtens

Cover design: A. Scholtens

© A. Scholtens

February 2023

Inhoud

Preface

This book provides a comprehensive overview of PKI, covering its key components, architecture, operations, applications, and limitations. It is suitable for beginners who want to learn the basics of PKI and its role in securing digital communications.

The book is full of examples and each chapter ends with questions and exercises to check the acquired knowledge.

You will find the answers at the back of this book.

Learning new things can be a satisfying experience. I therefore hope that you will enjoy reading this book.

Chapter 1: Introduction to Public Key Infrastructure (PKI)

This chapter provides a comprehensive introduction to PKI, its definition, history, key components, and use cases. The questions and exercises are designed to reinforce the concepts learned in this chapter and help readers understand PKI better.

1.1 Definition and Overview

Public Key Infrastructure (PKI) is a comprehensive and integrated system that enables secure communication over the Internet. It involves the use of cryptographic techniques, digital certificates, and certificate authorities (CAs) to establish a trusted and secure relationship between parties.

PKI enables the secure exchange of information between parties by providing three essential security services: confidentiality, integrity, and authenticity. Confidentiality refers to the protection of sensitive information from unauthorized access or disclosure. Integrity refers to the assurance that the information has not been altered during transmission. Authenticity refers to the assurance that the information comes from a trusted source and has not been tampered with.

PKI is designed to ensure the secure exchange of information by establishing a trust relationship between parties. This trust relationship is established by verifying the identity of the parties and issuing digital certificates that contain information about their identities and public keys. The digital certificates serve as a form of digital identification, allowing parties to verify each other's identities and establish secure communications.

Public Key Infrastructure provides a secure communication infrastructure for exchanging information over the Internet. It uses cryptographic techniques, digital certificates, and certificate authorities to establish trust and ensure the confidentiality, integrity, and authenticity of data and information exchanged between parties.

1.2 Historical Background

The concept of public-key cryptography was first introduced in the 1970s and marked a significant milestone in the field of cryptography. Before public-key cryptography, symmetric cryptography was the dominant method of encryption. Symmetric cryptography used a single key for both encryption and decryption, which created several challenges when it came to secure communication over a network.

Public-key cryptography, on the other hand, uses a pair of keys, one public and one private, to encrypt and decrypt information. The public key can be shared freely with anyone, and the private key must be kept secret. This type of cryptography solves many of the challenges posed by symmetric cryptography and makes secure communication over a network much more manageable.

As the use of public-key cryptography grew, so did the need for a framework to manage and distribute public keys. This led to the development of Public Key Infrastructure (PKI), which was created to provide a secure and scalable system for managing public keys and ensuring the secure exchange of information.

PKI has been widely adopted for various applications, including secure email, web transactions, and other secure communications over the Internet. It provides a comprehensive and integrated system for verifying the identity of parties, issuing digital certificates, and establishing secure communication. PKI has become an essential component of modern secure communication infrastructure, and its use continues to grow as the need for secure communication increases.

Public Key Infrastructure has its roots in the 1970s, when public-key cryptography was first introduced. It was developed to manage and distribute public keys and provide a framework for secure communication. Over the years, PKI has been widely adopted for secure communication over the Internet and has become an essential component of modern secure communication infrastructure..

1.3 Key Components of PKI

PKI is a complex system that involves several key components to ensure the secure exchange of information. These components are essential to the functioning of PKI and include:

1. Certificate Authorities (CA): Certificate Authorities (CAs) are organizations that are responsible for verifying the identity of parties and issuing digital certificates. CAs play a crucial role in PKI as they provide the foundation of trust upon which secure communication is built. CAs are typically trusted third parties that use rigorous authentication processes to verify the identity of parties before issuing certificates.

2. Digital Certificates: Digital certificates are electronic documents that contain information about an entity's identity and public key. Digital certificates serve as a form of digital identification and are used to verify the identity of parties in secure communications. They contain information such as the entity's name, public key, and the name of the issuing CA. Digital certificates are used to establish trust and provide the basis for secure communication.

3. Certificate Revocation Lists (CRL): Certificate Revocation Lists (CRLs) are lists of revoked certificates. Revoked certificates are certificates that are no longer considered valid due to various reasons, such as the private key being compromised or the certificate holder's identity being disputed. CRLs play an

important role in PKI as they allow parties to verify the validity of digital certificates before establishing secure communications.

4. Certificate Policies (CP): Certificate Policies (CPs) are sets of rules and procedures that govern the issuance and management of certificates. CPs provide a framework for CAs to follow when issuing and managing certificates, ensuring consistency and integrity in the PKI system. CPs define the procedures for verifying the identity of certificate holders, issuing certificates, revoking certificates, and managing certificate lifecycles.

So, the key components of PKI include Certificate Authorities (CAs), Digital Certificates, Certificate Revocation Lists (CRLs), and Certificate Policies (CPs). These components work together to establish a secure and trusted communication infrastructure, allowing parties to securely exchange information over the Internet.

1.4 Use Cases of PKI

PKI has a wide range of use cases and is used in many different industries and applications. Two of the most common use cases of PKI are secure email and web communications.

1. Secure email: PKI is widely used to provide secure email communication. When using PKI for email, digital certificates are used to verify the identity of the sender and to encrypt the message being sent. This ensures that only the intended

recipient can read the message and that the sender's identity cannot be forged.

2. Web communications: PKI is also used to provide secure web communications, such as secure online transactions and secure browsing. When using PKI for web communications, digital certificates are used to verify the identity of the website and to encrypt the communication between the user's browser and the website. This provides a secure and trusted communication channel, protecting sensitive information such as credit card numbers and personal information.

Public Key Infrastructure has several use cases, with secure email and web communications being two of the most common. PKI provides a secure and trusted communication infrastructure, allowing parties to securely exchange information over the Internet. The use of PKI continues to grow as the need for secure communication increases, and it has become an essential component of modern communication infrastructure.

1.5 Secure network communications

PKI is widely used to provide secure network communications, such as virtual private network (VPN) connections and secure shell (SSH) connections. When using PKI for network communications, digital certificates are used to verify the identity of the connecting parties and to encrypt the communication. This provides a secure and trusted communication channel, protecting sensitive information and ensuring that only authorized parties can access the network.

Secure network communications is an important use case of Public Key Infrastructure. PKI provides a secure and trusted communication infrastructure, allowing parties to securely exchange information over the Internet. The use of PKI continues to grow as the need for secure communication increases, and it has become an essential component of modern communication infrastructure.

1.6 Digital signatures and document security

1. Digital signatures: PKI is widely used to provide digital signatures, which are electronic versions of a traditional handwritten signature. Digital signatures use public-key cryptography to verify the identity of the signer and to ensure the integrity of the document. When using PKI for digital signatures, digital certificates are used to verify the identity of the signer and to secure the signature.

2. Document security: PKI is also used to provide secure document storage and exchange. When using PKI for document security, digital certificates are used to encrypt the document and to verify the identity of parties who have access to the document. This provides a secure and trusted way to store and exchange sensitive information, such as confidential business documents or personal health records.

Public Key Infrastructure provides a secure and trusted infrastructure for digital signatures and document security, allowing parties to securely store and exchange sensitive information. The use of PKI continues to grow as the need for secure communication and information storage increases, and it has become an essential component of modern communication and information security infrastructure.

1.7 Secure e-commerce transactions

Secure e-commerce transactions: PKI is widely used to provide secure e-commerce transactions, such as online banking and shopping. When using PKI for e-commerce transactions, digital certificates are used to verify the identity of the parties involved and to secure the transaction. This provides a secure and trusted environment for e-commerce transactions, protecting sensitive information such as credit card numbers and personal information.

Secure payment systems: PKI is also used to secure payment systems, such as credit card transactions and online payments. When using PKI for payment systems, digital certificates are used to verify the identity of the parties involved and to secure the transaction. This provides a secure and trusted environment for payments, protecting sensitive information such as credit card numbers and personal information.

Public Key Infrastructure provides a secure and trusted infrastructure for e-commerce transactions and payments, allowing parties to securely conduct online transactions and protect sensitive information. The use of PKI continues to grow as the need for secure e-commerce transactions increases, and it has become an essential component of modern e-commerce infrastructure.

1.8 Secure software distribution

Secure software distribution: PKI is used to secure the distribution of software, such as operating systems, applications, and firmware. When using PKI for software distribution, digital certificates are used to verify the identity of the software publisher and to secure the software distribution. This provides a secure and trusted way to distribute software, ensuring that only trusted sources can distribute software and that the software has not been tampered with during distribution.

Software updates: PKI is also used to secure software updates, ensuring that updates come from trusted sources and have not been tampered with during distribution. When using PKI for software updates, digital certificates are used to verify the identity of the software publisher and to secure the software update. This provides a secure and trusted way to distribute software updates, ensuring that only trusted sources can distribute updates and that updates have not been tampered with during distribution.

Public Key Infrastructure provides a secure and trusted infrastructure for software distribution, allowing software publishers to securely distribute software and software updates and ensuring that only trusted sources can distribute software and updates. The use of PKI continues to grow as the need for secure software distribution increases, and it has become an essential component of modern software distribution infrastructure.

Chapter 1: Questions and Exercises

1. What is the purpose of PKI?

2. Can you give an example of how PKI is used for secure email?

3. What are the key components of PKI?

4. Can you name a few use cases of PKI?

5. What is the difference between public-key cryptography and symmetric cryptography?

6. Why is it important for Certificate Authorities (CAs) to verify the identity of parties before issuing digital certificates?

7. What is a Certificate Revocation List (CRL) and what is its purpose?

8. What is the role of Certificate Policies (CPs) in PKI?

9. How does PKI provide secure e-commerce transactions?

Chapter 2: Understanding Cryptography and Cryptographic Algorithms

Cryptography is a technique used to secure communication by transforming data into a secure form that can only be read by authorized parties. It has been used for centuries to protect sensitive information, and has become increasingly important with the rise of electronic communication and the need for secure online transactions. Cryptography is used to ensure the confidentiality, meaning that the contents of a message are kept secret from unauthorized parties. It is also used to ensure the integrity of data, meaning that the contents of a message are not altered in transit. Additionally, cryptography can be used to provide authenticity, meaning that the sender and receiver of a message can be confident of each other's identities. In summary, cryptography is a key tool for secure communication, and helps to ensure that sensitive information is protected from unauthorized access, tampering, or misuse.

2.1 Symmetric and Asymmetric Cryptography

Symmetric and Asymmetric Cryptography Cryptography can be divided into two main types: symmetric and asymmetric. Symmetric cryptography, also known as secret-key cryptography, uses a single key for both encryption and decryption. This means that the same key must be shared by both the sender and the receiver of a message. This key must be kept secret, as if it falls into the wrong hands, the security of the encrypted data can be compromised.

Asymmetric cryptography, on the other hand, uses a pair of keys, one public and one private, for encryption and decryption. The public key is used to encrypt a message, while the private key is used to decrypt it. The public key can be freely shared, as it is only used for encryption. The private key must be kept secret, as it is used for decryption and must be used to sign digital signatures. Asymmetric cryptography provides greater security than symmetric cryptography, as the keys are not shared and can be used for separate functions. Additionally, asymmetric cryptography can be used to verify the authenticity of a message, as the private key can be used to create a digital signature that can be verified by the public key.

2.2 Hash Functions

Hash functions are an important component of cryptography and play a key role in ensuring the integrity of data. A hash function takes an input, such as a message, and produces a fixed-size output, known as a hash or digest. The output of a hash function is typically a string of characters that represents the input data in a condensed form.

Hash functions have several important properties that make them useful for cryptography. Firstly, hash functions are deterministic, meaning that given the same input, the same output will always be produced. Secondly, hash functions are one-way, meaning that it is infeasible to determine the input data from the hash. Finally, hash functions are collision-resistant, meaning that it is infeasible to find two different inputs that produce the same output.

These properties make hash functions useful for ensuring the integrity of data and verifying the authenticity of digital signatures. For example, if a message is transmitted from one party to another, the hash of the message can be computed and sent along with the message. The recipient of the message can then compute the hash of the received message and compare it to the original hash. If the two hashes match, then the recipient can be confident that the message has not been tampered with during transmission. Similarly, hash functions can be used to verify digital signatures, by computing the hash of the signed message and comparing it to the hash that is contained within the digital signature.

2.3 Digital Signatures

Digital signatures also play an important role in PKI, as they are used to secure electronic transactions, such as e-commerce and financial transactions, by providing a way to verify the authenticity of a message and the identity of the sender. Digital signatures are created using a combination of the sender's private key and a hash function, which creates a unique, fixed-size output that is then encrypted using the sender's private key. When a recipient receives the signed message, they can use the sender's public key to verify the digital signature and ensure that the message has not been tampered with. In this way, digital signatures provide a secure and efficient way to establish trust in electronic communications.

Questions and exercises chapter 2

1. Match the definition:

   a. Symmetric cryptography

   b. Asymmetric cryptography

   c. Hash function

   d. Digital signature

   i. Uses a single key for encryption and decryption

   ii. Uses a pair of keys for encryption and decryption

   iii. Produces a fixed-size output based on the input message

   iv. Verifies the authenticity of digital data

2. Fill in the blanks:

   Cryptography is the practice of secure communication. It involves transforming data into a secure form that can only be read by authorized parties. Cryptography is used to ensure the confidentiality, integrity, and ______________ of data and information.

3. What is the input and output of a hash function?

4. True or False: Digital signatures use symmetric cryptography.

5. Write a brief description of the steps involved in using a digital signature to verify the authenticity of digital data.

6. What is the difference between symmetric cryptography and asymmetric cryptography?

7. Can you provide an example of a use case for hash functions?

8. How does a digital signature prove the identity of the signer and the authenticity of the signed data?

9. Why is cryptography important for secure communication?

10. Can you explain the purpose of a hash function in cryptography?

Chapter 3: Public Key Infrastructure Architecture

Introduction

Public Key Infrastructure is a complex and dynamic system that provides secure communication over the Internet. PKI architecture plays a critical role in ensuring the confidentiality, integrity, and authenticity of information exchanged between parties. In this chapter, we will explore the different components of PKI architecture, including Certificate Authorities (CA), certification hierarchy, Certificate Revocation Lists (CRL), Certificate Policies (CP), and trust models.

3.1 Certificate Authorities (CA)

Certificate Authorities (CA) are the most important part of the PKI architecture. A certificate authority is a trusted third-party organization responsible for verifying the identity of parties and issuing digital certificates. The digital certificates issued by CAs contain information about an entity's identity and public key. CAs play a critical role in PKI by providing a secure way to distribute public keys and establish trust between parties.

3.2 Certification Hierarchy

Certification hierarchy refers to the structure of CAs and the relationships between them. Typically, a root CA is at the top of a certification hierarchy, followed by intermediate CAs, and finally end-entity CAs. The structure of the hierarchy is based on trust relationships, where the top level CA is known as the root CA and the intermediate and lower level CAs are known as subordinate CAs. The root CA is trusted by all parties in the hierarchy and is responsible for verifying the identity of the subordinate CAs. The intermediate CAs are responsible for issuing certificates to end entity CAs. The end entity CAs are responsible for issuing certificates to end users and organizations. This hierarchical structure provides a secure way to manage and distribute certificates and to ensure the authenticity of public keys.

3.3 Certificate Revocation Lists (CRL)

Certificate Revocation Lists (CRLs) are lists of revoked certificates. CRLs are important in PKI because they provide a way to quickly revoke certificates that are no longer valid. This is especially important for revoking certificates that have been compromised or stolen. CRLs can be checked by relying parties to ensure that the certificate used is still valid and has not been revoked.

3.4 Certificate Policies (CPs)

A certificate policy (CP) is a set of rules and procedures governing the issuance and management of certificates in a PKI. CPs define the criteria for issuing and revoking certificates, the methods for verifying the identity of certificate holders, and the responsibilities of the parties involved in the PKI. CPs are an important aspect of PKI because they ensure the security and reliability of the digital certificates used in secure communications.

3.5 Trust Models In PKI

Trust models define the trust relationships between entities, such as certificate holders and certificate authorities (CAs). There are several trust models used in PKI, including the hierarchical trust model, the web of trust model, and the bridge trust model. Each trust model defines different methods of establishing and maintaining trust between parties, and choosing the right trust model is critical to the success of a PKI implementation.

Exercises and Questions Chapter 3

1. Explain the role of a Certificate Authority (CA) in PKI.

2. What is the purpose of a Certificate Revocation List (CRL) in PKI?

3. Draw a diagram to illustrate the relationship between the root CA, intermediate CAs, and end-entity certificates in a certificate hierarchy.

4. Create a sample Certificate Policy document that outlines the rules and procedures for issuing, managing, and revoking digital certificates.

5. Research the different trust models used in PKI, such as trust-on-first-use, web-of-trust, and hierarchical trust models. Summarize the pros and cons of each model.

6. Write a scenario in which a certificate revocation list (CRL) would be used to revoke a digital certificate. Explain why it's important to have an up-to-date CRL.

7. Describe the difference between a root CA and an intermediate CA. What is the significance of the root CA's private key in PKI?

8. Explain the importance of certificate policies in PKI and why it is necessary for organizations to have a certificate policy in place.

9. Discuss the process of certificate issuance in PKI, including the steps involved in verifying the identity of the entity requesting

the certificate, and how a digital certificate is created and signed by a CA.

10. Analyze the difference between certificate-based authentication and username/password authentication in terms of security, ease of use, and scalability.

11. Investigate and compare the different types of CAs, such as root CAs, commercial CAs, and enterprise CAs, and provide examples of their use cases.

12. Develop a case study on how a PKI architecture can be used to secure online transactions in e-commerce, including the use of digital certificates and certificate revocation lists.

Chapter 4: Certificate Management

Certificate management is a crucial aspect of Public Key Infrastructure (PKI) as it ensures the secure and efficient operation of digital certificates throughout their entire lifecycle. Certificate management involves the issuance, renewal, reissuance, and revocation of digital certificates to ensure that they remain valid and secure.

4.1 Certificate Issuance and Management

Certificate issuance is the process of creating and distributing digital certificates to end-entities. The certificate issuance process starts with the end-entity submitting a certificate request to the Certificate Authority (CA), which includes the end-entity's public key and identity information. The CA then verifies the end-entity's identity and, if the end-entity is deemed trustworthy, issues a digital certificate containing the end-entity's public key and identity information. The certificate is then securely transmitted to the end-entity.

Once the certificate is issued, it must be managed to ensure that it remains valid and secure. This involves monitoring the certificate's expiration date and renewing the certificate if necessary. It also involves revoking the certificate if it is no longer needed or if the end-entity's identity or public key changes.

4.2 Certificate Renewal and Reissuance

Certificate renewal is the process of obtaining a new digital certificate before the current certificate expires. Renewal is necessary because digital certificates have a finite lifespan, typically one or two years, to ensure that the public key remains secure and up-to-date. The certificate renewal process is similar to the certificate issuance process, but with the added step of verifying that the end-entity's identity and public key have not changed since the last certificate was issued.

Reissuance is the process of issuing a new certificate when the end-entity's identity or public key has changed. This could be due to a change in the end-entity's name or address, for example, or a change in the end-entity's public key. The reissuance process is similar to the certificate issuance process, but with the added step of revoking the previous certificate.

4.3 Certificate Revocation

Certificate revocation is the process of invalidating a digital certificate. This is necessary when the end-entity's identity or public key changes or when the certificate is no longer needed. Certificate revocation is performed by the CA, which updates its Certificate Revocation List (CRL) with information about the revoked certificate. The CRL is then made available to all parties that use the CA's digital certificates, allowing them to verify that a certificate is still valid before relying on it.

Exercises and Questions Chapter 4

1. Write a scenario in which a certificate renewal would be necessary. What are the steps involved in the renewal process?
2. What happens if a certificate is not renewed before it expires?
3. Why is certificate reissuance necessary and what is the process for reissuing a certificate?
4. Create a flowchart to illustrate the process of certificate revocation.
5. Explain the importance of having an up-to-date Certificate Revocation List (CRL) in PKI. How does the CRL ensure the security of digital certificates?

Chapter 5: PKI Deployment and Operation

PKI implementation involves a number of steps, including the planning and preparation phase, the selection of a deployment scenario, and the ongoing operation and maintenance of the PKI system.

In the planning and preparation phase, organizations need to consider their specific requirements and determine the most appropriate PKI solution for their needs. This may include an assessment of their existing network infrastructure and an analysis of the risks and threats they face.

Once the planning and preparation phase is complete, organizations must select a PKI deployment scenario that meets their requirements. Common PKI deployment scenarios include a standalone PKI deployment, where the organization manages its own PKI system, or a managed PKI deployment, where a third-party service provider manages the PKI system on behalf of the organization.

Once a PKI system has been implemented, organizations must ensure that it is properly maintained and managed. This includes continuous monitoring of the system, updating the certificate revocation list (CRL), and managing certificate renewal and reissue processes. In addition, organizations must ensure that their PKI system is kept up-to-date with the latest security patches and software updates.

In this chapter, we provide a comprehensive overview of the key steps in deploying and operating PKI, including planning and preparation, deployment scenarios, and ongoing use and maintenance. Whether you are a novice or an experienced PKI administrator, this chapter will give you the information and guidance you need to implement and use a secure and effective PKI system.

5.1 Planning and Preparation

Plan and prepare

The planning and preparation phase of the PKI implementation is crucial to its success. It is important to take the time to fully understand the organization's requirements and the types of digital certificates that will be used. For example, you need to determine the number of Certificate Authorities (CAs) that will be required.

During this phase, it is also important to consider factors such as the security of the system, the scalability of the infrastructure, and the costs associated with deploying and maintaining the PKI system. This includes conducting a risk assessment to identify potential security threats and developing a security plan to mitigate those threats.

In addition to these technical considerations, organizations must also establish policies and procedures for certificate issuance, management, renewal, revocation, and other aspects of PKI operation. This includes defining roles and responsibilities for different individuals and departments, establishing security standards and guidelines, and determining the frequency and methods for conducting regular security audits. It is also important to develop a disaster recovery plan in case of security breaches or system failures.

In addition, organizations must consider the cost of the PKI system, including the cost of hardware, software, maintenance, and support. They must also consider the time required to plan, test and deploy the system, as well as the ongoing costs of operating and maintaining the system over time.

PKI implementation therefore requires careful consideration and good planning.

5.2 PKI Deployment Scenarios

PKI deployment scenarios can vary depending on the size and complexity of the organization. Some common deployment scenarios include:

1. Stand-alone PKI: A stand-alone PKI is a single-CA deployment in which a single CA is responsible for issuing and managing digital certificates. This deployment scenario is suitable for small organizations with simple certificate requirements.

2. Hierarchical PKI: A hierarchical PKI is a multi-CA deployment in which the root CA issues certificates to intermediate CAs, which in turn issue certificates to end-entities. This deployment scenario is suitable for organizations with complex certificate requirements and is more scalable than a stand-alone PKI.

3. Hybrid PKI: A hybrid PKI is a combination of stand-alone and hierarchical PKI deployment scenarios. This deployment scenario is suitable for organizations that require a combination of simple and complex certificate requirements.

5.3 PKI Operations and Maintenance

Additionally, regular software updates and patches should be applied to ensure that the PKI system is up to date and protected against the latest security threats. PKI administrators must also monitor the system for any potential security incidents and be prepared to respond quickly and effectively in the event of a security breach. Furthermore, they should have plans in place for disaster recovery and business continuity, to minimize the impact of any disruptions to the PKI system.

It is also important to implement a thorough training program for all users of the PKI system, to ensure that they understand how to use the system securely and are aware of their responsibilities in protecting the security of the digital certificates. Regular review and update of the policies and procedures for PKI operations and maintenance is also crucial to ensure that the system remains secure and effective over time.

In summary, the operation and maintenance of a PKI system is a continuous process that requires ongoing attention and investment to ensure the security and reliability of digital certificates.

Understanding the different deployment scenarios and the steps involved in PKI operation and maintenance will help ensure the security and reliability of digital certificates in your organization.

Exercises and Questions Chapter 5

1. Explain the key steps involved in PKI deployment and operation. What is the importance of careful planning and preparation before deploying a PKI system?

2. What is the purpose of identifying the types of digital certificates that will be used in PKI deployment?

3. What are the security requirements for a PKI system?

4. What is the purpose of performing regular security audits in PKI deployment and operation?

5. Why is it important to implement procedures for the safe storage of the private keys used for signing and issuing digital certificates?

6. Write a scenario in which a certificate revocation list (CRL) would be updated.

7. Research the different PKI deployment scenarios, such as a single root CA, multiple root CAs, and hierarchical CAs. Summarize the pros and cons of each scenario.

Chapter 6: Applications of PKI

Public Key Infrastructure has numerous applications in various industries. In this chapter, we will explore the different ways in which PKI is used to enhance security in email and web communications, secure network communications, and digital signatures and document security.

6.1 Secure Email and Web Communications

Secure email and web communications is a crucial area that benefits greatly from the use of PKI. In secure email communications, digital certificates are used to encrypt the contents of the emails, making it nearly impossible for anyone to access the information without authorization. This ensures the confidentiality of sensitive information, such as financial data or personal information, and provides peace of mind to the sender and receiver of the email.

In web communications, digital certificates are used to authenticate the identity of a website. This is important because it provides assurance to the user that they are communicating with the intended website and not a fake or malicious one. Digital certificates are also used to establish secure connections to the website, such as through the use of HTTPS, which protects against man-in-the-middle attacks and other forms of eavesdropping. By using digital certificates in these applications, PKI helps to ensure the security and privacy of online communications.

6.2 Secure Network Communications

In addition to encryption, PKI can also be used for secure authentication of network devices, such as routers and switches, and for secure authorization of network access. This helps to prevent unauthorized access to sensitive network resources and to ensure that only trusted users and devices have access to the network. PKI can also be used to secure virtual private network (VPN) communications, ensuring that the VPN connections are encrypted and secure against unauthorized access. The use of digital certificates in secure network communications helps to provide a high level of security for the data transmitted over the network, protecting against threats such as eavesdropping, tampering, and data theft.

6.3 Digital Signatures and Document

PKI provides a secure and efficient way to sign and verify electronic documents, reducing the risk of fraud and providing an added layer of trust in digital transactions. With the use of digital certificates, users can securely sign, verify and exchange sensitive information, including contracts, financial documents and legal agreements. The use of digital signatures and document security solutions based on PKI helps to ensure the integrity and authenticity of electronic documents, providing a secure and reliable alternative to traditional paper-based processes.

Exercises and Questions Chapter 6

1. What is the purpose of using digital certificates in email and web communications?

2. Explain how digital certificates are used to authenticate the identity of a website.

3. What is the purpose of using digital certificates in secure network communications?

4. How does PKI enhance the security of digital signatures and document security?

5. Research different digital signature technologies and explain the difference between them.

6. What is the significance of digital signatures in electronic commerce?

7. Write a scenario in which digital certificates and digital signatures are used to secure a financial transaction.

Chapter 7: Challenges and Limitations of PKI

Public Key Infrastructure (PKI) is a technology that plays a crucial role in ensuring the security of digital communications and transactions. However, despite its many benefits, PKI is not without its limitations and challenges. In this chapter, we will discuss the various limitations and challenges associated with PKI, including technical limitations, security limitations, and management limitations.

7.1 Technical Limitations

1. Complexity: One of the main technical limitations of PKI is its complexity. The technology behind PKI is based on complex mathematical algorithms and requires a deep understanding of cryptography and digital signatures to set up and manage effectively. This complexity can be a barrier to entry for many organizations, making it difficult for them to implement PKI effectively.

2. Scalability: PKI is designed to support large-scale digital communications, but it can become complex and challenging to manage as the number of users and devices increases. This can limit the scalability of PKI, making it difficult for organizations to support the growth of their digital infrastructure.

3. Interoperability: PKI relies on standard protocols and encryption methods to ensure interoperability between different systems

and devices. However, not all systems and devices are compatible with PKI, which can create compatibility issues and limit the ability of organizations to integrate PKI with their existing infrastructure.

4. Performance: PKI can impact the performance of digital systems and devices, as encryption and decryption can be resource-intensive processes. This can limit the efficiency of PKI and make it difficult to use in real-time applications, such as video conferencing or online gaming.

7.2 Security Limitations

1. Vulnerability to Attack: PKI is not immune to attack, and digital certificates and other components of PKI can be stolen or compromised. This can result in unauthorized access to sensitive information, such as email communications and financial data.

2. Certificate Revocation: Certificate revocation is a process that allows certificate authorities to revoke digital certificates that have been compromised or that are no longer valid. However, this process can be time-consuming and may not be effective in preventing unauthorized access to sensitive information.

3. Human Error: PKI relies on the actions of humans, and mistakes can be made that result in security breaches. For example, employees may use weak passwords, lose digital certificates, or

accidentally share sensitive information with unauthorized individuals.

4. Key Management: PKI relies on secure management of cryptographic keys, and the loss or compromise of these keys can severely impact the security of digital communications and transactions. This makes key management a critical challenge for organizations using PKI, and requires them to implement robust security measures to protect their keys.

5. Certificate Management: Digital certificates are a fundamental component of PKI, and managing these certificates effectively can be challenging. Organizations need to ensure that certificates are issued and managed securely, and that they are not vulnerable to fraud or counterfeiting.

7.3 Management Limitations

1. Maintenance: PKI requires ongoing maintenance and support, which can be time-consuming and expensive for organizations. This can limit the ability of organizations to keep up with the changing needs of their digital infrastructure, and can make it difficult for them to adopt new technologies and applications.

2. Cost: Implementing PKI can be expensive, as it requires the purchase of digital certificates, certificate authorities, and other components. The cost of PKI can also increase over time as

organizations need to renew digital certificates, replace outdated hardware, and upgrade software.

3. Human Error: PKI is only as secure as the people who manage it, and human error can be a significant challenge. This can include misconfigurations, forgotten passwords, or even theft of cryptographic keys. Organizations need to be aware of these risks and implement robust security measures to minimize the impact of human error.

PKI is a powerful technology that provides many benefits for secure communication, digital signatures, and document security. However, it is important to be aware of the challenges and limitations of PKI to ensure that it is implemented and used effectively. By understanding the technical, security, and management limitations of PKI, organizations can make informed decisions about its use and can ensure its continued security and reliability.

Exercises and Questions Chapter 7

1. Multiple Choice Question: What is the primary technical limitation of PKI?

   A. Difficulty in generating private keys

   B. Complexity of certificate management

   C. Lack of standardization

   D. Dependence on trusted third parties

2. True or False: One of the security limitations of PKI is the risk of compromise of private keys.

3. Fill in the Blank: One of the management limitations of PKI is the need for frequent ____________ of digital certificates.

   A. Creation

   B. Renewal

   C. Verification

   D. Validation

4. Short Answer: What is the significance of certificate revocation lists (CRLs) in PKI?

5. Matching Exercise: Match the following PKI limitations with their descriptions.

    A. Technical Limitations

    B. Security Limitations

    C. Management Limitations

    i Risk of private key compromise

    ii Difficulty in certificate management

    iii Lack of standardization

6. Short Answer: What is the role of a certificate authority (CA) in PKI and what are the limitations associated with it?

7. Scenario-Based Exercise: Imagine that you work for a company that wants to implement PKI for secure communication. What steps would you take to mitigate the limitations of PKI and ensure the security of the system?

Chapter 8: Conclusion

8.1 Summary

Summary of Key Points PKI, or Public Key Infrastructure, is a complex system of digital certificates, certificate authorities, and encryption algorithms used to provide secure online communications, digital signatures, and secure storage of sensitive documents. PKI has numerous applications in areas such as secure email, web communications, network communications, digital signatures and document security.

8.2 Future of PKI

PKI has proven to be an essential tool for secure online communication and digital transactions, and its importance is only set to grow as the world becomes increasingly digital. In the future, PKI will likely play an even larger role in securing the internet of things, blockchain technology, and other emerging technologies. It is also likely that new, more advanced encryption algorithms will be developed, further improving the security and privacy of PKI-based systems.

8.3 Final Thoughts and Recommendations

PKI can be a complex system to understand, but it is a critical component of modern security and privacy systems. It is important to understand its capabilities, limitations, and best practices to be able to make informed decisions about its use. It is recommended to seek expert advice and resources for implementation and management of PKI systems to ensure optimal security and functionality.

Exercises and Questions Chapter 8

1. Explain the purpose of PKI in one sentence.

2. What are some key applications of PKI?

3. How does PKI improve the security of online communications and digital transactions?

4. What do you think will be the future of PKI and why?

5. What are the technical limitations of PKI?

6. What are the security limitations of PKI?

7. What are some best practices for implementing and managing PKI systems?

Answers to the Questions and Exercises

Questions and Exercises Chapter 1

1. What is the purpose of PKI?

   The purpose of PKI is to provide secure communication over the Internet by establishing a trust relationship between parties. PKI is used to ensure the confidentiality, integrity, and authenticity of data and information exchanged between parties.

2. Can you give an example of how PKI is used for secure email?

   For example, when using PKI for secure email, digital certificates are used to verify the identity of the email sender and to encrypt the email message. The recipient of the email can use the public key in the sender's digital certificate to verify the sender's identity and to decrypt the message. This provides a secure and trusted way to send and receive email messages, ensuring that only the intended recipient can read the message and that the message has not been tampered with during transit.

3. What are the key components of PKI?

   The key components of PKI include: Certificate Authorities (CA), Digital Certificates, Certificate Revocation Lists (CRL), and Certificate Policies (CP).

4. Can you name a few use cases of PKI?

   A few use cases of PKI include: secure email and web communications, secure network communications, digital signatures and document security, secure e-commerce transactions, and secure software distribution.

5. What is the difference between public-key cryptography and symmetric cryptography?

   Public-key cryptography uses a pair of keys, one public and one private, to encrypt and decrypt information. Symmetric cryptography uses a single key for both encryption and decryption.

6. Why is it important for Certificate Authorities (CAs) to verify the identity of parties before issuing digital certificates?

   It is important for CAs to verify the identity of parties before issuing digital certificates because digital certificates are used to establish trust between parties. If a CA issues a digital certificate to an entity that is not who it claims to be, it undermines the trust that is established through the use of digital certificates.

7. What is a Certificate Revocation List (CRL) and what is its purpose?

   A Certificate Revocation List (CRL) is a list of revoked certificates. Its purpose is to allow parties to determine whether a digital certificate is still valid. If a certificate has been revoked, it is no longer considered trustworthy and should not be used.

8. What is the role of Certificate Policies (CPs) in PKI?

Certificate Policies (CPs) are sets of rules and procedures that govern the issuance and management of certificates. They define the requirements for the issuance of certificates, the methods for verifying the identity of parties, and the procedures for revoking certificates. CPs are important for ensuring the consistent and secure operation of PKI.

9. How does PKI provide secure e-commerce transactions?

PKI provides secure e-commerce transactions by using digital certificates to verify the identity of parties involved in the transaction and to encrypt the information exchanged during the transaction. This ensures that sensitive information, such as credit card numbers, is protected from unauthorized access and that the parties involved in the transaction can trust each other.

Questions and Exercises Chapter 2

1. Match the definition:

a. i. Symmetric cryptography uses a single key for encryption and decryption

b. ii. Asymmetric cryptography uses a pair of keys for encryption and decryption

c. iii. Hash function produces a fixed-size output based on the input message

d. iv. Digital signature verifies the authenticity of digital data

2   Fill in the blanks: Answer: authenticity

3. What is the input and output of a hash function?

   Answer: The input of a hash function is a message, and the output is a fixed-size output known as a hash or digest.

4. True or False: Digital signatures use symmetric cryptography.

   Answer: False. Digital signatures use asymmetric cryptography.

5. Write a brief description of the steps involved in using a digital signature to verify the authenticity of digital data.

   Answer: The steps involved in using a digital signature to verify the authenticity of digital data are:

   1. The signer generates a signature using their private key and the data to be signed.

2. The signature and the signed data are transmitted to the recipient.

3. The recipient uses the signer's public key to verify the signature and ensure that the signed data has not been tampered with.

4. If the signature is verified, the recipient can trust that the signed data is authentic and from the signer.

6. What is the difference between symmetric cryptography and asymmetric cryptography?

   Symmetric cryptography uses a single key for both encryption and decryption, while asymmetric cryptography uses a pair of keys, one public and one private, for encryption and decryption.

7. Can you provide an example of a use case for hash functions?

   An example of a use case for hash functions is in digital signatures. Hash functions can be used to generate a unique, fixed-size output from a message that can be used to verify the integrity of the message. If the original message changes, the hash value will change, allowing the recipient to determine if the message has been tampered with.

8. How does a digital signature prove the identity of the signer and the authenticity of the signed data?

   A digital signature proves the identity of the signer and the authenticity of the signed data by using asymmetric cryptography. The signature is generated by the signer using their private key, and can be verified using the signer's public key. The public key ensures that the signature was created by the corresponding private key and that the data has not been altered.

9. Why is cryptography important for secure communication? Cryptography is important for secure communication because it ensures the confidentiality, integrity, and authenticity of data and information. Cryptography provides a way to secure data in transit and to prevent unauthorized access, tampering, or theft of sensitive information.

10. Can you explain the purpose of a hash function in cryptography? The purpose of a hash function in cryptography is to ensure the integrity of data and to verify the authenticity of digital signatures. Hash functions take an input (also known as a message) and produce a fixed-size output (also known as a hash or digest). This output can be used to verify that the data has not been altered, and that the signature was created by the signer's private key.

Questions and Exercises Chapter 3

1. Explain the role of a Certificate Authority (CA) in PKI.

The role of a Certificate Authority (CA) in PKI is to verify the identity of parties and issue digital certificates that contain information about the entity's identity and public key. The CA acts as a trusted third-party organization that provides a secure way to distribute public keys and establish trust between parties in a network. By issuing digital certificates, the CA helps ensure the authenticity and security of communications between parties.

2 What is the purpose of a Certificate Revocation List (CRL) in PKI?

The purpose of a Certificate Revocation List (CRL) in PKI is to provide a list of revoked certificates. If a certificate is no longer valid for any reason, such as if the entity's private key is compromised or the entity is no longer authorized to use the certificate, it is added to the CRL. The CRL helps to ensure that revoked certificates are not used to establish trust between parties and that secure communications are not compromised by invalid certificates. The CRL is periodically updated by the CA and made available to parties in the network.

3. Draw a diagram to illustrate the relationship between the root CA, intermediate CAs, and end-entity certificates in a certificate hierarchy.

Diagram to illustrate the relationship between the root CA, intermediate CAs, and end-entity certificates in a certificate hierarchy:

Root CA

    |

    |

    Intermediate CA

    |

    |

    End-Entity Certificates

4. Create a sample Certificate Policy document that outlines the rules and procedures for issuing, managing, and revoking digital certificates.

   Sample Certificate Policy document:

   Certificate Policy for XYZ Inc.

   1. Introduction

   This policy outlines the rules and procedures for issuing, managing, and revoking digital certificates within XYZ Inc.

   2. Certificate Issuance

The XYZ CA will issue certificates to individuals and entities that meet the following criteria:

a. The entity must provide valid identification and proof of their identity.

b. The entity must provide a public key that will be used in the digital certificate.

c. The entity must agree to comply with this certificate policy and any applicable laws and regulations.

3. Certificate Management

The XYZ CA will be responsible for maintaining the accuracy and validity of all digital certificates issued. This includes:

a. Regularly checking the status of certificates and revoking any that are no longer valid.

b. Providing certificate revocation lists (CRLs) to ensure that revoked certificates are no longer trusted.

c. Keeping records of all issued certificates for a minimum of 7 years.

4. Certificate Revocation

Certificates may be revoked for the following reasons:

a. The private key associated with the certificate has been compromised.

b. The identity information in the certificate is no longer accurate.

c. The entity is no longer authorized to use the certificate.

5. Trust Model

The XYZ CA will use a hierarchical trust model, where the root CA is at the top of the hierarchy and intermediate CAs are used to issue certificates to end-entities. This ensures that all certificates are verified by a trusted third-party and the end-entity certificate is only issued after the identity of the entity has been verified.

6. Disclaimer

This certificate policy is subject to change without notice. Use of a digital certificate from XYZ Inc. constitutes acceptance of this policy and any changes made to it.

5. Research the different trust models used in PKI, such as trust-on-first-use, web-of-trust, and hierarchical trust models. Summarize the pros and cons of each model.

Trust models used in PKI:

i. Trust-on-First-Use (TOFU) - In this model, trust is established the first time a certificate is used. If the certificate is later revoked or becomes invalid, the user will not be notified.

Pros: Simple and easy to implement.

Cons: Lack of ongoing trust verification and no notification of certificate revocation.

ii. Web-of-Trust - In this model, trust is established through a network of trusted individuals who have verified each other's identities.

Pros: Trust is established through personal relationships, making it a more secure model.

Cons: Difficult to establish and maintain a network of trust, and it can be challenging to determine who to trust.

iii. Hierarchical Trust Model - In this model, trust is established through a chain of trust, starting with a trusted root CA and extending down to intermediate CAs and end-entity certificates.

Pros: Provides a clear chain of trust, making it easier to verify the authenticity of certificates.

Cons: Relies on the security and reliability of the root CA, making it important to ensure the root CA is secure.

6. Write a scenario in which a certificate revocation list (CRL) would be used to revoke a digital certificate. Explain why it's important to have an up-to-date CRL.

Scenario: A digital certificate for a user's email account has been compromised. To revoke the compromised certificate, the user submits a revocation request to the issuing CA. The CA verifies the request and adds the revoked certificate to the CRL. The CRL is then distributed to all parties who need to verify the validity of the certificate.

It's important to have an up-to-date CRL because revoked certificates may be used in malicious activities such as phishing or impersonation attacks. By checking the CRL, parties can ensure they are not accepting a revoked certificate, thus reducing the risk of such attacks.

7. Describe the difference between a root CA and an intermediate CA. What is the significance of the root CA's private key in PKI?

A root CA is the top-level entity in a certificate hierarchy and is responsible for issuing certificates to intermediate CAs. An intermediate CA is a lower-level entity in the hierarchy and is responsible for issuing certificates to end-entity certificates. The root CA's private key is critical in PKI because it is used to sign the public keys of other CAs, establishing trust between parties in the hierarchy. The private key must be kept secure and protected from unauthorized access to maintain the security and integrity of the certificate hierarchy.

8. Explain the importance of certificate policies in PKI and why it is necessary for organizations
to have a certificate policy in place.

Certificate policies outline the rules and procedures for issuing, managing, and revoking digital certificates. It is necessary for organizations to have a certificate policy in place as it helps establish trust in the digital certificates used for secure communication. The certificate policy ensures that the certificates issued by the organization are valid, trustworthy, and have not been revoked.

9. Discuss the process of certificate issuance in PKI, including the steps involved in verifying the
identity of the entity requesting the certificate, and how a digital certificate is created and
signed by a CA.

The certificate issuance process in PKI starts with the entity requesting a certificate from a CA. The entity provides information about its identity and public key, which the CA verifies. The CA then creates the digital certificate and signs it using its private key. The digital certificate is then returned to the entity, who can use it for secure communication.

10. Analyze the difference between certificate-based authentication and username/password
authentication in terms of security, ease of use, and scalability.

Certificate-based authentication is more secure than username/password authentication because it provides strong proof of identity. Certificate-based authentication is also easier to use and more scalable than username/password authentication, as it eliminates the need for users to remember multiple usernames and passwords.

11. Investigate and compare the different types of CAs, such as root CAs, commercial CAs, and
enterprise CAs, and provide examples of their use cases.

Root CAs are trusted third-party organizations that issue digital certificates to other CAs and end-entities. Commercial CAs are CAs that offer digital certificate services to individuals and organizations for a fee. Enterprise CAs are CAs that are maintained by organizations for their internal use. Each type of CA has its own use case, and organizations should choose the type of CA that best meets their needs.

12. Develop a case study on how a PKI architecture can be used to secure online transactions in

e-commerce, including the use of digital certificates and certificate revocation lists.

A PKI architecture can be used to secure online transactions in e-commerce by using digital certificates and certificate revocation lists. The customer and the merchant both have digital certificates that are used to establish trust in the transaction. The customer's digital certificate is used to verify their identity, and the merchant's digital certificate is used to verify their authenticity. The certificate revocation list is used to ensure that the digital certificates used in the transaction have not been revoked.

Questions and Exercises Chapter 4

1. Write a scenario in which a certificate renewal would be necessary. What are the steps involved in the renewal process?

   Certificate renewal is necessary when a certificate reaches its expiration date or when information in the certificate changes, such as the entity's name or address. The steps involved in the renewal process include:

   - Verifying the identity of the certificate owner

   - Generating a new certificate request

   - Submitting the certificate request to the Certificate Authority (CA)

   - Verifying the authenticity of the certificate request

   - Issuing a new certificate with updated information

2. What happens if a certificate is not renewed before it expires?

   If a certificate is not renewed before it expires, it will no longer be considered a valid certificate and will not be trusted by relying parties. This means that secure communication using that certificate will no longer be possible.

3. Why is certificate reissuance necessary and what is the process for reissuing a certificate?

Certificate reissuance is necessary when a certificate becomes compromised or when information in the certificate changes that cannot be updated through a renewal process. The process for reissuing a certificate involves:

- Revoking the old certificate

- Verifying the identity of the certificate owner

- Generating a new certificate request

- Submitting the certificate request to the CA

- Verifying the authenticity of the certificate request

- Issuing a new certificate with updated information

4. Create a flowchart to illustrate the process of certificate revocation.

The process of certificate revocation involves:

- Determining that a certificate is no longer valid or trustworthy

- Revoking the certificate

- Updating the Certificate Revocation List (CRL) with information about the revoked certificate

- Distributing the updated CRL to relying parties

5. Explain the importance of having an up-to-date Certificate Revocation List (CRL) in PKI. How does the CRL ensure the security of digital certificates?

An up-to-date CRL is important in PKI because it helps ensure the security of digital certificates by providing information about revoked certificates. If a relying party receives a certificate that is listed on the CRL, they can be confident that the certificate is no longer valid and should not be trusted. The CRL helps to prevent the use of revoked certificates in secure communication, which can compromise the security of the communication.

1. Explain the key steps involved in PKI deployment and operation. What is the importance of careful planning and preparation before deploying a PKI system?

   Answer: Before deploying a PKI system, it is important to assess the organization's needs and determine the requirements for the PKI deployment. This includes identifying the types of digital certificates that will be used, determining the number of certificate authorities (CAs) needed, selecting the appropriate hardware and software components, and considering the security requirements for the PKI system. The operation and maintenance of a PKI system are critical to ensuring the security and reliability of the digital certificates. This includes tasks such as issuing and managing digital certificates, updating the certificate revocation list (CRL), performing regular security audits to ensure the security of the PKI system, and implementing procedures for the safe storage of the private keys used for signing and issuing digital certificates.

2. What is the purpose of identifying the types of digital certificates that will be used in PKI deployment?

   Answer: Identifying the types of digital certificates that will be used in PKI deployment helps determine the number of certificate authorities (CAs) needed and the appropriate hardware and software components required for the deployment. It also helps determine the security requirements for the PKI system, such as the type of secure storage needed for the private keys.

3. What are the security requirements for a PKI system?

   Answer: The security requirements for a PKI system include the need for secure storage of the private keys, the use of secure protocols for communication, and the need for physical security controls to protect against unauthorized access.

4. What is the purpose of performing regular security audits in PKI deployment and operation?

   Answer: Performing regular security audits in PKI deployment and operation is important to ensure the security of the PKI system. It helps identify any vulnerabilities or potential threats to the system and allows for timely remediation to maintain the security and reliability of the digital certificates.

5. Why is it important to implement procedures for the safe storage of the private keys used for signing and issuing digital certificates?

   Answer: Implementing procedures for the safe storage of the private keys used for signing and issuing digital certificates is important to protect against unauthorized access. If the private keys were to fall into the wrong hands, it could result in the issuance of fraudulent digital certificates, compromising the security and reliability of the PKI system.

6. Write a scenario in which a certificate revocation list (CRL) would be updated.

   Answer: A certificate revocation list (CRL) would be updated in the event that a digital certificate is revoked. This could occur if the private key associated with the certificate is lost or stolen, if the identity information contained in the certificate is found to be incorrect, or if the certificate is used for unauthorized purposes. Updating the CRL ensures that the revoked certificate is no longer trusted and helps maintain the security and reliability of the PKI system.

7. Research the different PKI deployment scenarios, such as a single root CA, multiple root CAs, and hierarchical CAs. Summarize the pros and cons of each scenario.

   Answer: A single root CA scenario involves having a single trusted third-party organization responsible for issuing digital certificates and verifying the identity of parties. A multiple root CA scenario involves having multiple trusted third-party organizations responsible for issuing digital certificates. A hierarchical CA scenario involves having multiple levels of CAs, with a root CA at the top and intermediate CAs below, responsible for issuing digital certificates. The pros and cons of each scenario will depend on the specific needs and requirements of the organization deploying the PKI system.

Questions and Exercises Chapter 6

1. What is the purpose of using digital certificates in email and web communications?

   The purpose of using digital certificates in email and web communications is to provide security and privacy for the information being transmitted. Digital certificates are used to encrypt emails, ensuring that the contents of the emails are protected against unauthorized access. In web communications, digital certificates are used to authenticate the identity of the website, ensuring that the website is trustworthy and secure.

2. Explain how digital certificates are used to authenticate the identity of a website.
   Digital certificates are used to authenticate the identity of a website by confirming the authenticity of the website's domain name and verifying the identity of the entity that owns or operates the website. This helps to prevent phishing attacks and other forms of online fraud, and provides users with confidence that they are communicating with a legitimate website.

3. What is the purpose of using digital certificates in secure network communications?

   The purpose of using digital certificates in secure network communications is to ensure the confidentiality and integrity of data transmitted over the network. Digital certificates are used to encrypt network communications, providing protection against unauthorized access, tampering, and eavesdropping. Digital certificates are also used to authenticate the identity of devices on the network, ensuring that only trusted devices can access the network.

4. How does PKI enhance the security of digital signatures and document security?

PKI enhances the security of digital signatures and document security by providing a secure and reliable method for digitally signing and verifying electronic documents. Digital signatures allow the authenticity of electronic documents to be verified, ensuring that the document has not been altered in any way. PKI also provides secure storage solutions for sensitive documents, helping to ensure that they are protected against unauthorized access.

5. Research different digital signature technologies and explain the difference between them.

Different digital signature technologies include:

- Asymmetric cryptography-based digital signatures, where a public key is used to sign a document and a private key is used to verify the signature.

- Hash-based digital signatures, where a message digest is created from the document and then signed with a private key.

- Symmetric cryptography-based digital signatures, where a shared secret key is used to both sign and verify the signature.

6. What is the significance of digital signatures in electronic commerce?

The significance of digital signatures in electronic commerce is that they provide a secure and reliable way to sign and verify electronic transactions, reducing the risk of fraud and providing an added layer of trust in digital transactions. Digital signatures also help to streamline and automate many manual business processes, reducing the need for paper-based documentation and increasing efficiency.

7. Write a scenario in which digital certificates and digital signatures are used to secure a financial transaction.

A scenario in which digital certificates and digital signatures are used to secure a financial transaction could involve a consumer making an online purchase from an e-commerce website. The consumer's browser would use the digital certificate of the e-commerce website to confirm its identity and establish a secure connection using HTTPS. The consumer would then securely enter their payment information, and the e-commerce website would use a digital signature to securely sign and confirm the transaction. The payment processing company would then use the digital signature to verify the authenticity of the transaction and securely process the payment.

Questions and Exercises Chapter 7

1   Multiple Choice Question: What is the primary technical limitation of PKI?

C. Lack of standardization

2. True

3. B. Renewal

4. Short Answer: What is the significance of certificate revocation lists (CRLs) in PKI? Answer: Certificate revocation lists (CRLs) are used in PKI to ensure that revoked digital certificates are not used for secure communications.

5. Matching Exercise: Match the following PKI limitations with their descriptions.
A. iii
B. i
C. ii

6. Short Answer: What is the role of a certificate authority (CA) in PKI and what are the limitations associated with it?

Answer: A certificate authority (CA) is responsible for issuing digital certificates and providing trusted third-party validation in PKI. One of the limitations of CA is that it can become a single point of failure, increasing the risk of compromise.

7. Scenario-Based Exercise: Imagine that you work for a company that wants to implement PKI for secure communication. What steps would you take to mitigate the limitations of PKI and ensure the security of the system?

   Answer: To mitigate the limitations of PKI, the following steps can be taken:

   - Choose a standard that is widely recognized and supported

   - Use strong encryption algorithms to secure private keys

   - Implement proper certificate management procedures, including regular renewal and revocation of certificates

   - Regularly monitor and review the system for any security vulnerabilities

   - Consider using multiple CAs for redundancy and to reduce the risk of a single point of failure.

Questions and Exercises Chapter 8

1. Explain the purpose of PKI in one sentence.

Answer: PKI is a system of digital certificates, certificate authorities, and encryption algorithms used to provide secure online communications, digital signatures, and secure storage of sensitive documents.

2. What are some key applications of PKI?

Answer: Key applications of PKI include secure email, web communications, network communications, digital signatures, and document security.

3. How does PKI improve the security of online communications and digital transactions? Answer: PKI improves the security of online communications and digital transactions by using encryption and digital certificates to authenticate the identity of users and websites, and to ensure the confidentiality, integrity, and authenticity of electronic documents and communications.

4. What do you think will be the future of PKI and why?

Answer: The future of PKI is likely to be shaped by new and emerging technologies, such as the internet of things and blockchain. As these technologies become more widespread, PKI will play an increasingly important role in securing digital transactions and communications.

5. What are the technical limitations of PKI?

Answer: Technical limitations of PKI include the complexity of the system, the need for regular maintenance and updates, and the cost of implementing and maintaining a PKI system.

6. What are the security limitations of PKI?

   Answer: Security limitations of PKI include the risk of certificate authority compromise, the risk of key compromise, and the need for regular maintenance and updates to keep the system secure.

7. What are some best practices for implementing and managing PKI systems?

   Answer: Some best practices for implementing and managing PKI systems include using trusted certificate authorities, regular security audits, using strong encryption algorithms, and implementing robust backup and recovery processes.

References and further reading

Books:

"Cryptography Engineering: Design Principles and Practical Applications" by Niels Ferguson, Bruce Schneier, and Tadayoshi Kohno.

"Applied Cryptography: Protocols, Algorithms, and Source Code in C" by Bruce Schneier.

"Cryptographic Security Architecture: Design and Verification" by Peter Gutmann.

Articles:

"A Brief Introduction to Public Key Infrastructure (PKI)" by Gary C. Kessler

"Public Key Infrastructure (PKI) Explained" by J.M. Smith

"Public Key Infrastructure (PKI) for Dummies" by Brian Chee

9 798215 252864